SHOT AND CAPTURED

PHOTOGRAPHS OF THE ROYAL SCOTS DRAGOON GUARDS BATTLEGROUP IN IRAQ 2003

TONY NICOLETTI
MAJOR AIDAN STEPHEN

SHOT AND CAPTURED
The Royal Scots Dragoon Guards Battlegroup in Iraq 2003

Published by the Scottish Daily Record,
and Sunday Mail Ltd,
One Central Quay, Glasgow G3 8DA.

Designed and edited by First Press Publishing,
One Central Quay, Glasgow G3 8DA.

ISBN 0-9544202-3-3

BLESMA – British Limbless Ex-Serviceman's Association – will benefit from profits made from this book

Her Majesty The Queen
Colonel in Chief
The Royal Scots Dragoon Guards

Her Majesty The Queen inspecting soldiers from The Royal Scots Dragoon Guards on a visit to the Regiment in 2002

THE following is an excerpt from a message by Her Majesty The Queen sent to members of the British Armed Forces on the day before the invasion of Iraq.

"May your mission be swift and decisive, your courage steady and true and your conduct in the highest traditions of your service both in waging war and bringing peace. My thoughts are with you all and with your families and friends who wait at home for news and pray for your safe return.

"At this moment in our nation's history, I would like to express my pride in you, the British service and civilian personnel deployed in the Gulf and in the vital supporting roles in this country and further afield.

"I have every confidence in your professionalism and commitment as you face the challenges before you."

The Colonel of The Regiment

YOU all know the adage: "A picture is worth a thousand words". How true this maxim is. This beautifully produced book records graphically the trials and tribulations of the gallant actions undertaken by members of The Royal Scots Dragoon Guards Battlegroup in Iraq between March and May 2003.

Beneath the glossy surface, the photographs tell a true and harsh story where man and machine had to endure the terror of war.

It is hard for us, sitting in a peace-time environment, to appreciate fully the hardships the Battlegroup had to suffer – sleep deprivation, fear, illness and the real threat of injury and death.

Any armoured vehicle is useless unless the team inside it is well trained and the men in that team or section have the courage and enthusiasm to fight. This book records, in a spectacular manner, how successful they were at responding to the clarion call of battle.

This is a story of men at war. Wars will never cease, grievous though that thought may be. The British nation, I submit, is lucky to have such fine soldiers.

This book is testimony to the courage, service, sacrifice and faith of those who served in The Royal Scots Dragoon Guards Battlegroup. I salute all those who were involved in its production, both photographer and soldier. I commend it to you.

Major General JMFC Hall, CB OBE
Colonel,
The Royal Scots Dragoon Guards

Managing Director,
Scottish Daily Record & Sunday Mail Ltd

IT is exceptionally rare to find a book that vividly portrays a moment of history. This is such a book. The journalist has a duty to cover the war, the soldier has a duty to fight it. When we embedded two of our journalists with the Royal Scots Dragoon Guards we wished to bring the news of their war to their families and friends who waited anxiously back home.

A partnership born in war has resulted in a strong association with Scotland's Cavalry, the Royal Scots Dragoon Guards, and the Daily Record, Scotland's biggest newspaper.

It is difficult to define with words the overwhelming achievements of our soldiers, to explain the courage and fear of the Iraqi civilians, to summarise those moments when tired and exhausted men faced each new day with a new strength.

These pictures offer an insight but they are also a memento, a record and a tribute. They are an "exact observation" from the view of a Daily Record photographer and from a soldier as seen through the lenses of their cameras.

I am delighted that the Daily Record is associated with the Royal Scots Dragoon Guards in defining that moment in history through the pages of this book.

MARK HOLLINSHEAD
Managing Director,
Scottish Daily Record
and Sunday Mail Ltd.

The Commanding Officer

THE enduring reality of any war is set in the minds of those who were there – every memory is recorded differently by individuals while history may ultimately compress or distort the details.

Within the same vehicle crew or fighting section, the recollections of a particular moment of war are radically diverse and the memories are stored in a very private "bank".

The photograph taken in a fraction of a second captures a reality as fast as the shot from a weapon can change a person's life.

But the lens, the skill and the artistic eye of the photographer are all as variable as those individual memories.

Until the era of digital photography, it was a reasonable assumption that the camera never lied. However, none of these digital images has been reconstructed or enhanced – they are all exact and honest observations that capture completely both the build-up in Kuwait and the operation in Southern Iraq.

This book is dedicated firstly to the soldiers and families of The Royal Scots Dragoon Guards and those attached to the Regiment during Operation TELIC.

Self-evidently, the liberation of Basrah and Southern Iraq could not have been achieved so successfully without the thorough dedication and professionalism shown by the soldiers represented in this pictorial history.

But, equally, we could not have managed what we did without the support of the families and administrative staff left at home who had to cope with the mounting anxiety as we deployed into Iraq to join battle in uncertain circumstances and for an indeterminate period.

This book is also dedicated to the journalists who deployed with the Battlegroup on Operation TELIC. They knew nothing of the military environment or what they were really letting themselves in for when they joined us.

This book is as much a tribute to their utter professionalism, determination and gallantry,

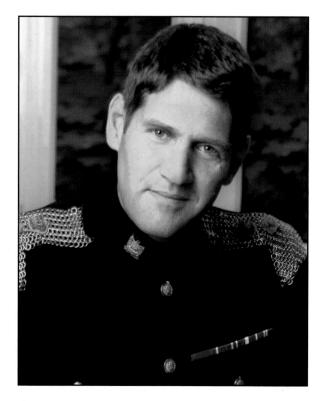

all of which are clearly reflected in the following pages.

Direct communication between soldiers and their families was impossible during this brief war but the images and written words provided by our embedded journalists did much to maintain the critical link between the fighting troops and the home base.

The journalists' exceptional achievements in the most testing and demanding of circumstances should not go unrecognised.

Finally, this book is dedicated to the memories of the two soldiers who did not return to their families with the remainder of the Battlegroup. They are Lance Corporal Ian Malone and Piper Christopher Muzvuru, both of whom were killed in action during the liberation of Basrah city – lest we forget.

Lt Col HH Blackman,
Commanding Officer,
Royal Scots Dragoon Guards

Introduction

THERE are so many times in life that we might wish we had a camera. Wartime is not necessarily a time to want to take photographs or to be able to do so – there are often more important things at hand.

The media covered the war in extraordinary detail. From the initial bombing of Baghdad to the liberation of Iraq, it was an endless stream of footage – the first truly 24/7 war on the television.

For many of the families left at home, this incessant coverage made it harder to bear and the imagination ran wild. For the soldiers in Iraq, the war outside their own little battle-space was hidden. They relied entirely on the radio and some belated print journalism.

Despite the drama, the horror and the absorbing reports that were all captured by daring cameramen and reporters, there will always be something missing – the photograph which gives time for reflection and the writer who has had time to reflect.

There is a certain luxury in looking at a moment of time that has been captured and shot by a camera and this book is much more about images than words.

Words give a brief outline of the events but the photographs provide more than any words ever can. Each one tells a story.

Not only do they portray the hardships and the humour, they also show the people of Iraq who we fought to liberate.

Our own losses are hard to bear but, under Saddam Hussein, the losses suffered by the Iraqi people were many times worse.

Major Aidan Stephen

9

Preparing for war

ON 20th January 2003, 7th Armoured Brigade (The Desert Rats) was warned to prepare for a possible deployment to Kuwait in anticipation of the potential liberation of Iraq. The Royal Scots Dragoon Guards was to form a Battlegroup with two squadrons of tanks (B and C Squadrons) and two companies of armoured infantry (Numbers 1 and 2 Companies of The Irish Guards).

A Squadron was detached to provide the armoured capability to The Black Watch Battlegroup.

Arriving in Kuwait in early March, the Battlegroup prepared for war. For some of the officers and soldiers in The Royal Scots Dragoon Guards it was a familiar place as the Regiment had earned two Battle Honours there during the 1991 Gulf War.

The heat and dust were a far cry from the freezing snow-covered training area in Germany on which the Battlegroup had recently trained.

Now the entire Battlegroup, with its tanks, infantry, engineers (31 Armoured Engineer Squadron from 32 Engineer Regiment) and artillery (C Battery from 3rd Royal Horse Artillery) had to adjust to the conditions and focus on the task at hand.

There was little time to prepare and the desert of northern Kuwait was full of Coalition troops and vehicles. Everyone needed to confirm the accuracy of their weapon systems and train thoroughly for the eventuality of war.

Supplies were shipped in and brought forward to the soldiers. It was a monumental logistical task and, despite various shortfalls, there was at least enough food and water.

With the combined array of satellites in the sky, bombers and laser-guided weapons, all the way down to the skills of a confident tank gunner, the Coalition was getting ready.

CHALLENGER 2 had been brought into service in 1998 by the Regiment. The crews knew that in their hands, the tank would silence not only the enemy but also the critics.

On the local Kuwaiti training area this confidence grew. The time to prepare was short but anticipated

setbacks and breakdowns turned out to be minimal.

With the vehicles up-armoured and training and zeroing complete, the operational ammunition was then loaded. The pace of life was frenetic – little time for food and little time to contemplate.

The threat of chemical or biological attack hung over Coalition troops – gas masks were always on the hip or over the face. With plans set and diplomatic exertions at an end, the Battlegroup prepared for war.

Dawn chorus: Corporal Johnston plays reveille. In Kuwait, a piper played each morning and evening to signify the beginning and end of day-time routine. This practice was continued in Iraq after the war.

Vital supplies: Boxes packed with medical equipment arrive in Kuwait (opposite page) but the extreme temperatures made storage difficult. The medical officer took a fridge and a generator into Iraq and was constantly harassed by thirsty soldiers hoping to store water at a temperature below 40C.

On the move: The tanks head to the Udairi Ranges for live firing – including a battle-run incorporating infantry, artillery, engineers and aviation

The Commanding Officer sets the standard.
A close shave every day was essential
– not just for smartness but so the gas mask
seal sat tight against the skin

Be prepared: Corporal Kennan, the Commanding Officer's radio operator, in the process of bore-sighting the gun to confirm accuracy prior to firing on the ranges.

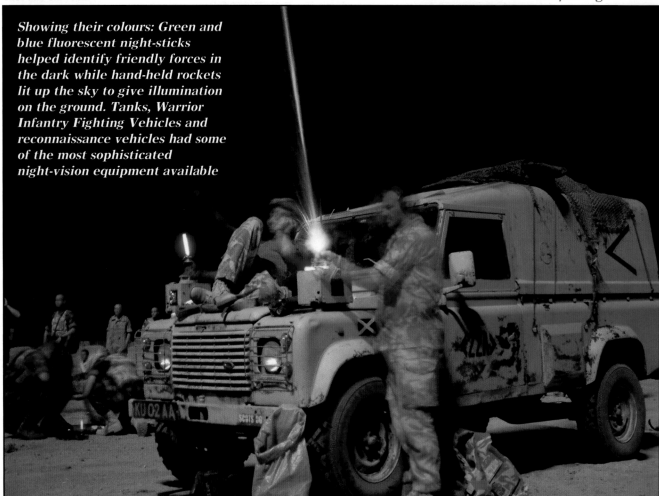

Showing their colours: Green and blue fluorescent night-sticks helped identify friendly forces in the dark while hand-held rockets lit up the sky to give illumination on the ground. Tanks, Warrior Infantry Fighting Vehicles and reconnaissance vehicles had some of the most sophisticated night-vision equipment available

Engine change: Essential preventative maintenance is carried out by Royal Electrical and Mechanical Engineers, who worked extremely long hours to keep the Battlegroup on the move

SCUD launch: The warning comes over the radio. The missile's destination, Kuwait. Everyone dons gas masks and looks for cover. There is a new sense of fear. A Sergeant Major tries the back of a Sultan Command Vehicle but discovers that a press of soldiers and an officer have already filled the space. Shouting through his gas mask, he makes a valid point and induces a laughing fit... "Look – it's a small bomb and a big planet. Will everyone stop panicking about the war!"

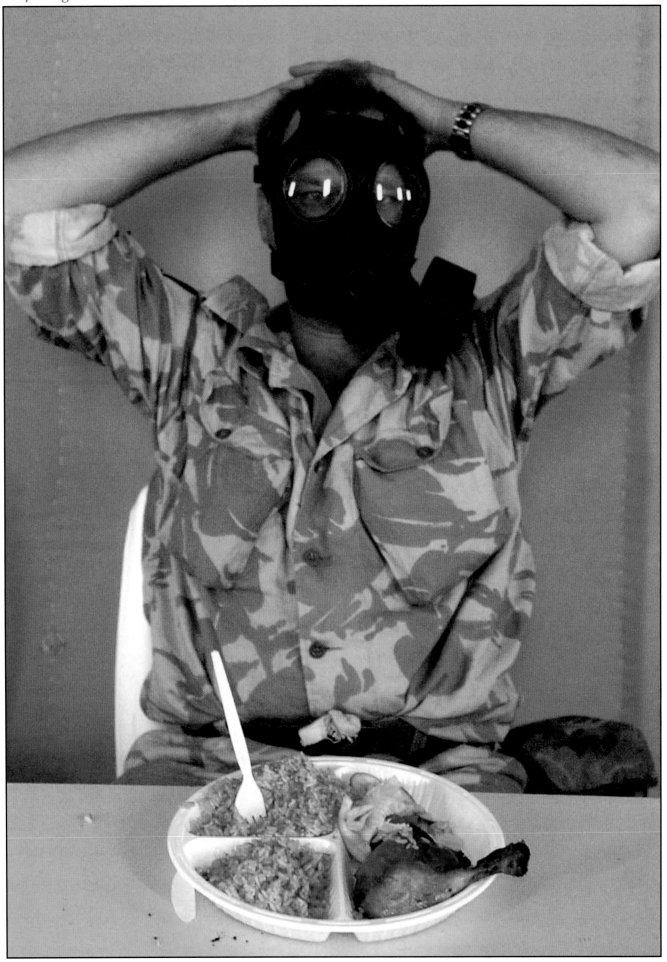

Group photo: The Battlegroup Officers have their photograph taken before leaving for Iraq

Swift into Iraq

ON March 19th, Reconnaissance Troop moved closer to the border to the Forward Assembly Area, ready to mark the route for the Battlegroup across a line in the sand and into Iraq. An early missile strike on Baghdad had started the war and, having received their orders, the Coalition push into Iraq was under way.

By March 21st, the Battlegroup was on one hour's notice to move. It had been the last to complete training in Kuwait – stormy weather had delayed the arrival of the vehicles – and it was initially allocated the task of Brigade Reserve.

By now the training and anticipation had fully "coiled the spring" of The Royal Scots Dragoon Guards Battlegroup and, when ordered to move, 200 vehicles drove north into Iraq faster than anyone had anticipated.

That first night inside Iraq under a hostile sky concentrated minds. The Battlegroup was soon tasked to move further north and relieve elements of 1st The Queen's Dragoon Guards beyond the Shat-Al-Basrah canal the following morning. The move was rapid and that night, in the marshes to the northwest of the city, the enemy met their first CHALLENGER 2. A rapid blocking position was placed by the Squadrons and small groups of enemy attacked with Rocket-Propelled Grenades, machine-gun fire and mortars.

Following intelligence that there was an imminent threat of encirclement by the enemy from the north, the Battlegroup moved to an area on Shaibah Airfield the next morning after a long and sleepless night. The enemy had taken a hard hit but commanders were eager to avoid collateral damage and it became increasingly obvious that the enemy was content to wait inside the city. The war was not going to end within 100 hours.

Order to advance: The Commanding Officer in his CHALLENGER 2 prepares to get the Battlegroup moving

In position: Reconnaissance Troop marks a junction and prepares to escort Battlegroup vehicles to the Iraqi border

Stop and search: Irish Guardsmen halt a civilian vehicle to search for weapons. The sky was full of smoke from deliberately-ignited oil pits and destroyed vehicles. It was to be our first sunset of many inside Iraq

First meeting: With hundreds of Coalition vehicles crossing into Iraq, it was not long before a minor traffic jam held up the Battlegroup convoy. Opposite, the first view of Iraq as Sergeant Major Gray swings open the door to let in some air. Stepping out of the vehicle, he crossed the road to hand some boiled sweets to a curious shepherd boy

Out of the blue: The third morning in Iraq breaks with a blue dawn. American troops joined the Battlegroup to provide a link-up with US air cover and support. Behind our temporary Headquarters was a battery of artillery. When they fired the first salvo that morning, the ground shook and the noise was deafening. There was a panicked rush for cover, until an "old sweat" pointed out the rounds were outgoing, not incoming. Everyone soon appreciated the difference

Daily Life

DAILY life was by no means normal. With the Battlegroup now at war, every hour held new challenges. Everyone had to be flexible, ready to move at a moment's notice and ready to fight the enemy.

There was such a rapid tempo to the war that it was imperative to be two steps ahead of the enemy, so that when required to react to a possible counter attack or incoming mortars, soldiers moved with a disciplined speed and did not allow the enemy to seize the initiative.

This constant pace was tiring and, amid the frenetic continuum of mental and physical pressure, the soldiers would take whatever time was available to eat, sleep or write home. For some, there were long spells of boredom, followed by periods of strain.

The dedicated professionalism of the soldiers was reinforced by one overwhelming characteristic – that extraordinarily British sense of humour and the ability to laugh in adversity.

In some of the very worst moments, someone would break the mood with a damning comment, punctuated with a stream of expletives and a sigh of resignation. Humour did not change the stark reality of the war, nor did it diminish the hardship – but it was a wonderful weapon to have at hand.

Order from disorder: A medic in a rubble-filled classroom at Basrah's Technical College. Initially, it had been occupied by the Fedayeen during the break-in to the city, but the college was quickly taken by the Battlegroup, who used its shattered classrooms as a forward operating base

Hot to handle: The daily temperatures averaged 35C but, as summer approached, there were days when the mercury went closer to 50C. The frequent dust storms made life particularly unpleasant. Water was a precious commodity for washing and bathing.
Over the page, six litres of water a day was issued to the soldiers

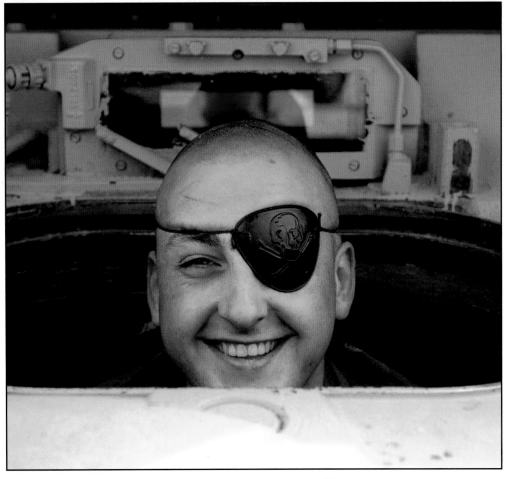

*Listening post:
The radios were
manned 24 hours a
day. Every message
was logged and staff
at Headquarters filled
30 books with details
of the transmissions*

Mothers' Day greetings: Some soldiers send a message home to their mums

Mothers' Day greetings: Some soldiers send a message home to their mums

Double exposure: The photographers took these near identical shots at exactly the same moment

Another chapter: The Provost Sergeant "Mad Pierre" Smith, right, sets up the Basrah Chapter of the Hell's Angels – as indicated on the door behind him

Grin and bear it: Trooper Cameron was due to leave the Army but extended his service to stay with the Regiment in Iraq. He's now a civilian but has threatened to return if the outside world is not to his liking.

Bomb disposal: Captured mortar rounds are off-loaded and moved to a demolition pit, left, as the Second-in-Command, Major Charlie Lambert, heads off for a cup of tea, right

The refugees

THE roads into Basrah were littered with burnt-out Iraqi vehicles and discarded equipment. Smoke still rose from oil pits and the Fedayeen were still in the city.

There were a number of bridges across the canals into the city and 7th Armoured Brigade dominated these routes from 23rd March.

The Royal Scots Dragoon Guards Battlegroup was called forward to conduct a relief-in-place with The Black Watch Battlegroup on 29th March. There had been continual fighting in the preceding days, but little sign of refugees. Although some locals chose to leave the city, the majority stayed.

But after one particularly heavy night of bombing hundreds left, perhaps sensing that a full attack was imminent.

The refugees (displaced civilians) were guided to camps for shelter and food. A steady stream also provided a wealth of information betraying those loyal to Saddam Hussein. As the intelligence picture became clearer, it was time to plan for entry into the city.

Planning for Battle

ORDERS groups ("O" Groups) were held twice daily or as the situation demanded. Detailed orders were given to sub-units within the Battlegroup, with all points leading to a focused and coordinated mission.

The Commanding Officer talked over his plans and his orders from Brigade round the map table with his staff prior to delivering his orders to his sub-unit commanders. The map table was a familiar focus to everyone.

It had been to Bosnia and Kosovo on operations and on exercises in Germany, Poland and Canada. It was the central hub of the Headquarters.

Tony Nicoletti's photograph of an "O" Group held in a bunker on Shaibah Airfield has become one of the most iconic images of the war.

Described by some as akin to an "Old Master's" painting, Tony has truly captured the moment.

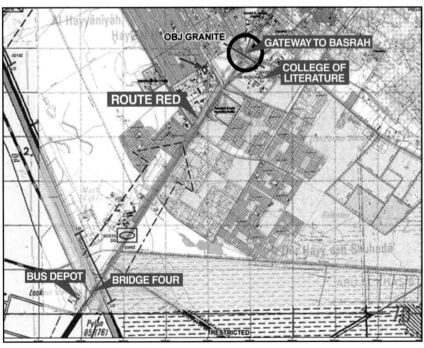

Previous page: Orders Group in an abandoned bunker at Shaibah Airfield – the Commanding Officer and staff wrestle with the complexities of supporting a possible Shi'ia uprising in Basrah.
Above: Major Chris Brannigan gives orders to B Squadron.
Left: A plans map of Basrah

Tsar Nicholas II

A hand-painted Icon of Tsar Nicholas II was presented to the regiment by the Caledonian Society of Moscow in 2001.

His Imperial Majesty Tsar Nicholas II was appointed Colonel in Chief of The Royal Scots Greys in 1895 by Her Majesty, Queen Victoria.

The Icon is taken on operations and was hung on the map board in Battlegroup Headquarters during the war.

Break

ONCE orders had been given, it was up to the officers and soldiers to carry out the mission. To gather intelligence and defeat the enemy, a series of probing raids pushed into the city suburbs.

With C Squadron redeployed in support of 3 Commando Brigade on the Al Faw Peninsula, it was left to B Squadron and Numbers 1 and 2 Companies of the Irish Guards to conduct these raids.

Two F-15E Strike Eagle ground-attack aircraft had bombed a Ba'ath Party headquarters in the centre of the city following high-level intelligence.

The resistance had subsequently reduced. The enemy presence was still

into Basrah

heavy but seemed to lack coordination.

A bus depot near the southern end of one of the bridges became a forward operating base for the Battlegroup.

Sporadic enemy mortar, sniper and artillery fire soon located our position. It was not uncommon for members of the Battlegroup to be awoken by a mortar round landing near their vehicles.

Meanwhile, A Squadron (as part of 1 Black Watch Battlegroup) had a narrow escape when a coordinated and accurate multi-barrelled rocket (BM-21) attack landed among their vehicles.

There were casualties but, remarkably, no fatalities. The steady destruction of the enemy positions continued through late March into early April.

The Battlegroup moved east into the outskirts of Basrah and set up a forward base in the Technical College.

The main road into Basrah was bordered by endless enemy bunker positions, which were steadily cleared during the raids.

As barricades were put in place, so they were destroyed. T-55 tanks still in the city were also engaged and steadily the enemy started to crumble.

By April 6th, the Battlegroups were raiding deep into the city, though it had not yet been determined when they would actually occupy the centre permanently.

Ultimately, though, April 6th became a "rolling maul", with The Desert Rats remaining in the city that night after a day of heavy fighting.

> **"As a driver I couldn't really see what was going on about us – but as we charged into Basrah,
> I could see rockets flying across us and the tank taking incoming fire.
> The adrenalin just took over"**
>
> TROOPER STUART HERKES
> – 'A' SQUADRON

Out of service: The bus depot near Bridge Four, the main access route into Basrah from the south

Taking the fight to the enemy

I N a bold and ambitious operation, C Squadron joined up with 3 Commando Brigade on the Al Faw Peninsula. At short notice, the Squadron moved to a ferry crossing.

Then they crossed the estuary by M3 ferry in the dark in negligible visibility (incidentally, the first operational deployment of M3 ferry) to attack into the flank of Iraqi Regular Army forces and link up with the Royal Marines.

Over the following days, C Squadron, under command of Major Johnny Biggart (pictured left), was involved in two significant tank battles. The headlines "14-0" covered the pages of national newspapers.

It was frustrating for our embedded journalists that the Squadron was so far away with such a big story unfolding. However, when one crew returned with a dented CHALLENGER 2, it became apparent that it had not been a complete walkover.

Crew members also described how the Fedayeen had held children in front of them as "human shields" as they moved from one firing position to another. The Squadron then returned to the Battlegroup for a rest but was soon involved again with the push into Basrah.

In the firing line: Opposite top, Sergeant Potter sits with his head in his hand with his crew and other members of B Squadron around him. They had just returned from a raid up the main road into the city and as far as the "Gateway to Basrah". Right, heavy calibre machine-gun rounds leave their mark on a stowage bin

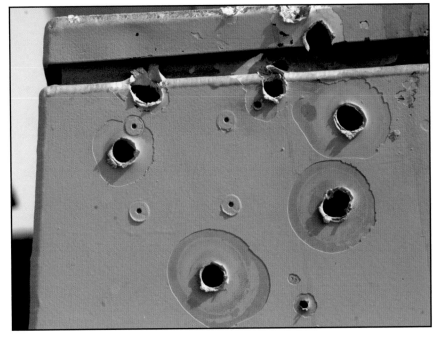

Bruised but not bowed: At least seven Rocket Propelled Grenades (RPGs) and one other missile hit the tank of Sergeant Baird and his crew. The tank was recovered by the gallant action of the Recovery Mechanics of the Light Aid Detachment and was operational within days

Still firing: One round hit this gunner's sight but with two others available, he was able to carry on shooting

TV interference: Although not part of the Battlegroup, A Squadron, led by Major Tim Brown (left), completed a raid into Basrah to destroy a TV and radio mast. Above, the Squadron Leader talks to the commanders after the raid to gather intelligence and discover what lessons had been learned

"It was one hell of a morning. I sat up in my sleeping bag and thought someone was taking a pounding – then there was an explosion just 30ft away. We dived into a tank ditch and sat listening to the thuds. It was really terrifying, a rude awakening to where I really was"

TROOPER CALLUM HOPE
– 'A' SQUADRON

Street battle

THE armour on CHALLENGER 2 and WARRIOR had saved many lives, but once the perimeter to an objective was secure it was necessary to get men on the ground to clear the area. As B Squadron Leader's tank broke down the gates to the College of Literature, dozens of Fedayeen emerged firing Rocket Propelled Grenades. The infantry companies of the Irish Guards deployed from behind the safety of their WARRIORS and engaged the enemy. Tony Nicoletti was the only embedded photographer there. These are some of his shots.

Large numbers of the enemy were cleared from bunkers, buildings and trenches. By last light, it was believed all of the Fedayeen had been cleared from the complex. A night-time defensive posture was adopted but, nonetheless, Piper Muzvuru and Lance Corporal Malone were killed by Fedayeen hiding in the university. Lance Sergeant Holland and Lance Corporal Martin were also injured. Basrah had now fallen after a long battle – but the deaths and injuries were an enormous blow for all.

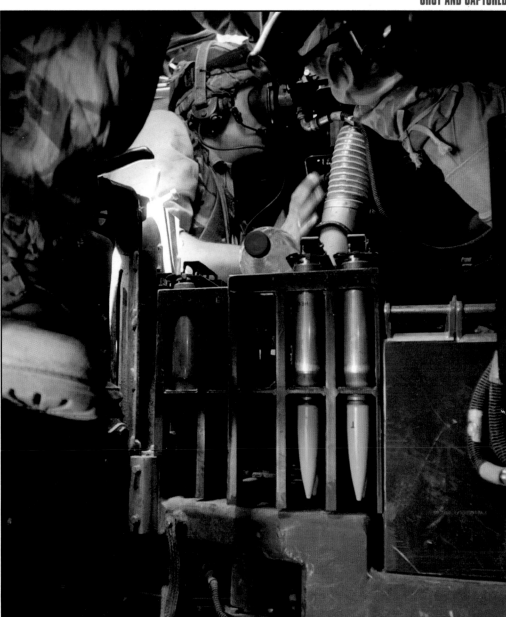

Danger at every turn: As the tanks rolled past, many of the Fedayeen fighters feigned death. They would then attempt to jump up onto the back of the tanks and attack our soldiers through the vehicle hatches

"Do you see that dead guy? He's the guy who tried to kill me. A lot of them were playing dead and he got up and brought his RPG to bear on me. The whole radio net was screaming 'Get down, RPG 20 metres from you' – but I'd no idea where he was. One of my colleagues shot him. I would've known nothing about it if I hadn't been saved."

CAPTAIN NIALL BRENNAN
– IRISH GUARDS

Basrah is liberated

THE battle for the "Gateway to Basrah" was over and the city was no longer host to an oppressive regime – April 7th was their day of liberation.

Concerns that significant numbers of enemy lay in the heart of the city were soon dismissed as hordes of children surrounded the soldiers and statues and murals of Saddam were torn down all over the city.

It was an extraordinary day.

The jubilation was everywhere and the only sign of unrest was when locals turned on the looters and started to stone them.

There was a genuine euphoria in the streets as the regime crumbled but patrolling and vehicle check-points became the routine.

The Battlegroup reorganised on April 11th, taking back A Squadron and assuming Egypt and Falcon Squadrons of the 2nd Royal Tank Regiment, and releasing the two Companies of Irish Guards to the command of the Black Watch Battlegroup.

The Brigade had more than 4,000 fighting troops in Basrah, surrounded by almost three million locals.

After years of propaganda and intimidation, many were terribly confused and frightened.

The regime had left deep scars and an absence of any truth. Trust came slowly, but the gratitude was immediate.

The soldiers had been mindful of the needs of the locals and thus the infrastructure had been left intact by the fighting.

Unfortunately, some facilities had been sabotaged by Fedayeen or looted by locals seeking to profit from the chaos.

The switch from war-fighting to peace-keeping was not an easy one to make.

With the cooperation of the locals and the expertise of military engineers and the International Committee of the Red Cross, fresh water began to flow again.

In all parts of the city, distribution points were set up, delivering millions of gallons of drinkable water to local people.

And during the hours of darkness, the looters started to return stolen items to the Mosques.

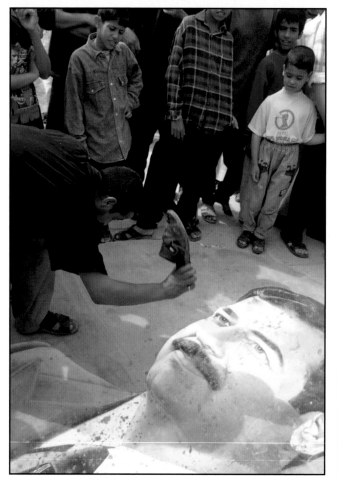

The Commanding Officer greets the locals on the road into Basrah

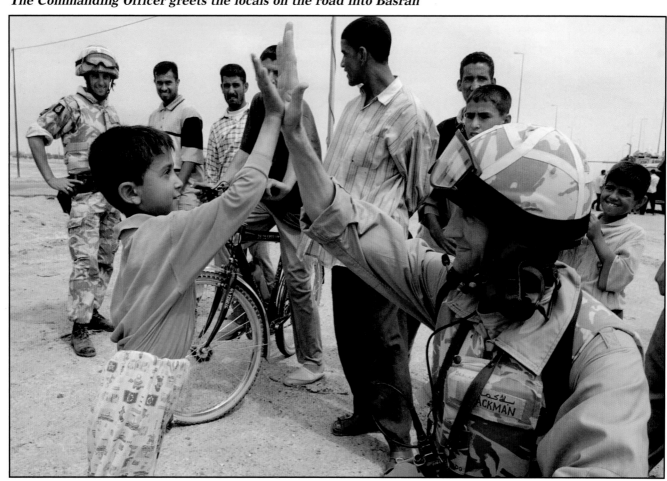

Human swarm: A commander from Reconnaissance Troop scratches his head as thousands of locals gather at a water distribution point he is guarding. There was constant vigilance for suicide bombers, as explosive vests had been found in the city

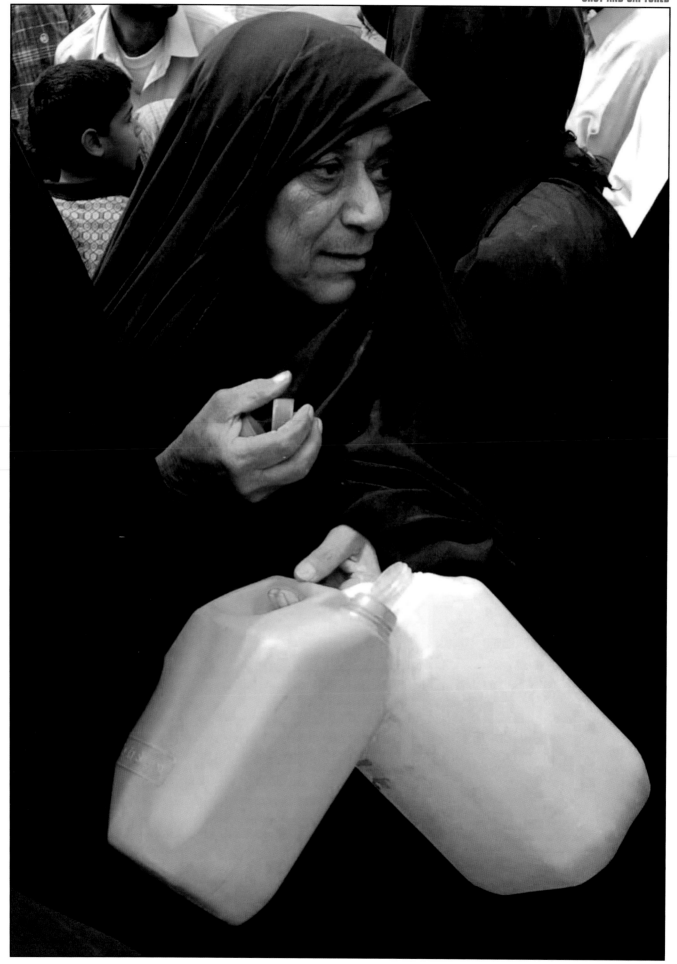

End of the fear: A poster of Saddam is ripped up, left. His eyes had already been burnt out with a cigarette

Preparing for action: Soldiers from Number 2 Company, Irish Guards, listen to the sound of gunfire as they prepare to reinforce another platoon. An armed bank robbery and two Fedayeen attempting to leave the city had come into contact with foot patrols. Lance Sergeant Giles had been shot in the chest and evacuated. The city was occupied by British troops, but criminals were determined to take advantage of the war. A robust approach brought this under control

Under cover: Battlegroup Headquarters relocated to Shaibah Airfield. The camouflage nets offered some shade from the searing heat

Whatever happens over the coming months, during those initial weeks there was an overwhelming outburst of gratitude from the population of Basrah. The people of Iraq now have a new hope.
In Basrah, there is a degree of freedom not previously dreamed of and, as ever, the future is for the children

The future of Basrah

'NEVER question what it is that you have done. Over the coming weeks and months, no matter what the politicians or people say, we are grateful and humbled by your sacrifices on our behalf.

Thirty years from now when I am an old man, my grandchildren will be enjoying a freedom and life that we could only dream of and it would not have been possible without your efforts. You have given us a possible future – it is up to us to make it work.'

Abdullah Al-Mahoud, speaking to the Commanding Officer at a meeting of sheiks and dignitaries on April 10th.

The Commanding Officer passed on these words to the Battlegroup to emphasise that their actions had made a real future possible for millions of strangers.

130

Back to school: The first day of school. By chance, Major Stephen came across this school of 400 immaculately-dressed children, opposite, just after it had re-opened. The teacher took him round every class and introduced him to the children. He returned a few days later and delivered all the sweets the Battlegroup could muster from the food parcels sent by relatives and friends

Maintaining traditions

Pipe Major's lament: Repairs are needed to the Pipe Major's bagpipes. They had been stowed in a box but were hit by a stray round in Iraq

ALTHOUGH in slightly difficult circumstances, St Patrick's Day was nonetheless celebrated by The Irish Guards in Kuwait before they deployed into Iraq.

The Royal Scots Dragoon Guards held a parade to remember the fallen from the Battle for Nunshigum.

Held on Shaibah Airfield after the liberation of Basrah, the parade served also to remember all those who had lost their lives during this conflict.

A few miles from the airfield in the middle of the desert, there was a memorial to those who had died in Iraq between 1914 and 1921.

It was visited by C Squadron in the days immediately before we departed Iraq to return to Germany.

Members of B Squadron, encouraged and led by their Light Aid Detachment, decided to march back to the Kuwaiti border, covering the 45 miles in less than 12 hours.

They raised almost £6,000 from other soldiers within the Brigade, and the money was given to BLESMA.

Proceeds from this book will go to the same cause.

On parade: The Regiment is called to attention for the Battle Honour of Nunshigum

Captured: C Squadron with an Iraqi T-55 tank

Markers for the fallen: There was surprisingly little damage to the memorial tablets, right, to commemorate those who died in Iraq between 1914 and 1921. The repair of the site was already under way as we left Iraq for Germany

*Parting shots: Members of Battlegroup
Headquarters, above, and the Regiment
forms up to receive flight details, below*

Coming home

THE Royal Scots Dragoon Guards returned home to Germany on 16th May 2003. They were met at Hannover Airport by Tony Nicoletti and Simon Houston from The Daily Record, who had both been "embedded" as accredited journalists with the Battlegroup during the war in Iraq and had travelled to Germany to cover our return.

The soldiers were piped "home" as they touched down again on European soil – each with their own thoughts and memories of their experiences in Iraq and eagerly awaiting their reunion with loved ones.

In the finest tradition

The Royal Scots Dragoon Guards

THE Royal Scots Dragoon Guards (SCOTS DG) are Scotland's senior Regiment and her only regular cavalry. The Regiment has a long, distinguished history having been founded in 1678 when King Charles II ordered that troops should be raised at the House of the Binns.

Shortly afterwards, these troops were united under a single command and became known as the Scots (or Royal North British) Dragoons, later to become known as The Royal Scots Greys.

In 1971, they amalgamated with the 3rd Carabiniers to form the current Regiment, The Royal Scots Dragoon Guards.

Both of these Regiments have long

and distinguished histories, taking part in many of the campaign and wars over the past three centuries.

Among these battle honours are Marlborough's campaigns, Wellington's famous battles, the Crimea, South Africa and the Two World Wars, as well as Northern Ireland and the Gulf War of 1991.

More recently, the Regiment has taken part in several peace-keeping operations in Bosnia and Kosovo.

Fifty-two of the Regiment's battle honours are displayed on the Regimental Standard.

Perhaps the most celebrated battle was Waterloo, where Sergeant Charles Ewart, during the famous charge of the Greys (pictured above) as part of the Union Brigade,

captured the Imperial Standard of the French 45th Regiment of Foot.

Thus the Eagle of Imperial France, together with the crossed carbines of the 3rd Carabiniers, form the Regiment's cap badge.

Another significant battle-honour is Nunshigum (part of the World War Two battle for the Japanese-held area of Imphal) when B Squadron 3rd Carabiniers, supported by the 1st Dogra Regiment, attacked and secured a hill vital to the security of the Allied Forces.

All the officers were killed during the initial attack, leaving the Squadron Sergeant Major to lead the Squadron until the enemy position was finally captured.

The Regiment is currently

(Carabiniers and Greys) 'Scotland's Cavalry'

stationed at Fallingbostel in Northern Germany, serving as part of the 7th Armoured Brigade (the 'Desert Rats' – a name originally given to its predecessor, 7th Armoured Division, during WW2 in the deserts of North Africa).

The Royal Scots Dragoon Guards were the first armoured regiment to receive the British Army's new main battle tank – CHALLENGER II – in 1998.

The Regiment completed its Training Year in late 2002 – involving exercises in Canada, Poland and Germany – and was then part of the UK's Lead Armoured Task Force (LATF) ready to deploy anywhere in the world at short notice.

Home Headquarters for the Regiment is Edinburgh Castle, which

also houses the Regimental Museum. The Regiment recruits primarily from Scotland although there are soldiers and officers from across the UK and the Commonwealth within its ranks.

The Regiment has a strong musical heritage and maintains its own Pipes and Drums that are ranked as one of the best in Scotland.

The Pipes and Drums have carried out many successful tours to all parts of the world, most recently spending eight weeks touring Australia, New Zealand and USA in late 2002.

They shot to fame in 1972 with their haunting rendition of "Amazing Grace" that reached No.1 in the UK charts. A new CD "Parallel Tracks" was released in November 2002 and features "Going Home" – a track with

Mark Knopfler (of Dire Straits fame) playing with the Pipes and Drums.

The Regimental slow march is "The Garb of Old Gaul" and the Quick March is "3DGs". The Pipe Marches are "My Home" and "Highland Laddie" respectively.

The Regiment maintains strong affiliations with The Windsor Regiment (Royal Canadian Armoured Corps), The 12th/16th Hunter River Lancers (Australian Army), 1st and 2nd Squadrons The New Zealand Scottish, The Natal Carbineers, Lothian and Borders Police, HMS Glasgow and HMS Vengeance.

Although battle tanks have replaced horses, the Cavalry spirit lives on and provides both inspiration and history for the modern Regiment.

Lest we forget

THIS book is dedicated to the memories of the two soldiers who did not return to their families with the remainder of the Battlegroup

LANCE CORPORAL IAN MALONE joined the 1st Battalion The Irish Guards in 1997. Having never previously left Ireland he joined the Battalion as it started its tour of Germany and he was to spend the majority of his career serving in Munster. During this time he visited more than 20 countries including Canada, The Oman, Kosovo, Poland and Korea.

Lance Corporal Malone was one of the best loved members of the Pipe Band and his sense of humour and love of life were legendary within Number Four Company (In Germany the Drums and Pipes formed Number 12 Platoon).

He was a natural member of a Platoon well known for their mischievous sense of humour and fun loving spirit and he will be irreplaceable amongst their ranks.

As an individual Lance Corporal Malone represented everything that makes the Micks so special. Dedicated both to the Battalion and to his friends he was a thinking man who readily absorbed himself in reading and who could play a mean game of chess (as several opponents found out to their cost). It was impossible not to like 'Molly' as he inevitable became known and his easy-going manner endeared him to all members of the Battalion.

One of Lance Corporal Malone's closest friends from his native Ballyfermot best summed him up with the words 'he was a very rounded guy with an electric personality.'

Lance Corporal Malone served on Operation TELIC in Number One Company, which played an integral role in securing Basrah in April this year. He was tragically killed whilst securing the Company's Area of Responsibility in the south of the city.

His funeral was remarkable for both the number of supporters present (more than 2000 people attended the funeral in Dublin) and for the first time since 1922 British Soldiers were given permission to march the streets of Dublin as part of his bearer party.

Molly will be greatly missed by the Battalion and all those who knew him. Molly died doing the job he loved.

In the Oman in 2001 he told RTE television: "At the end of the day I am just abroad doing a job. People are going on about Irishmen dying for freedom. That is a fair one, they did. But, they died to give men like me the freedom to choose what to do."

Our sympathy goes to his family and to his girlfriend Sarah Wolter.

PIPER CHRISTOPHER MUZVURU joined the 1st Battalion The Irish Guards in October 2001 and was immediately sent to the Pipe Band in Number Four Company. In so doing he became the first black Piper in the Regiment's history. Having completed his first piping course at the Army School of Piping he returned to the Battalion and was subsequently deployed on Operation TELIC as a member of Number One Company.

The circumstances of his joining the Micks are worth noting: whilst visiting the United Kingdom for the first time he was impressed by soldiers he had seen in London and found himself in a recruiting office on the point of signing up for the Royal Green Jackets. A keen eyed Irish Guards recruiting sergeant soon steered him away and

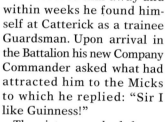

within weeks he found himself at Catterick as a trainee Guardsman. Upon arrival in the Battalion his new Company Commander asked what had attracted him to the Micks to which he replied: "Sir I like Guinness!"

The picture on the left was taken by an American journalist who interviewed Piper Muzvuru in Iraq. He told the journalist that what he really wanted was to play the pipes for Her Majesty The Queen. The very next day he was killed. Piper Muzvuru displayed a genuine talent for the Pipes and on the morning of his death played two Irish tunes on his chanter. He was a quiet individual, honest and well liked by his platoon. He always had a smile on his face.

Much was reported in the press about the Zimbabwean Government's refusal to allow Piper Muzvuru a burial in Zimbabwe. To the relief of his family and the Battalion this decision was subsequently rescinded.

In addition it should be noted that on the occasion of his repatriation to the United Kingdom some forty members of his family were waiting at RAF Brize Norton with the Regimental Lieutenant Colonel and Regimental Adjutant also in attendance. On that afternoon a Requiem Mass was said. Such a sad occasion was made brighter by the level of support and by the professionalism of the Royal Air Force.

Piper Muzvuru's death was a tragedy: he was a promising young man on the verge of a great career in the Micks. He will be sorely missed by the Battalion and particularly the Pipe Band who will doubtless toast him on the day they next play before the Queen.

Our sympathy goes to his family in Zimbabwe.

THE following personnel served with The Royal Scots Dragoon Guards Battlegroup in Iraq 2003

RANK	NAME	UNIT
LT COL	BLACKMAN	SCOTS DG
MAJ	BIGGART	SCOTS DG
MAJ	BRANNIGAN	SCOTS DG
MAJ	BROWN	SCOTS DG
MAJ	CUSHNIR	SCOTS DG
MAJ	FARRELL	1 IRISH GUARDS
MAJ	LAMBERT	SCOTS DG
MAJ	MACMULLEN	1 IRISH GUARDS
MAJ	ROBERTSON	SCOTS DG
MAJ	SCOTT	31 ARMD ENGR SQN
MAJ	STEPHEN	SCOTS DG
MAJ	WARNER	3 RHA
CAPT	AMBROSE	SCOTS DG
CAPT	BIANCONI	3 RHA
CAPT	BISHOP	SCOTS DG
CAPT	BRENNAN	1 IRISH GUARDS
CAPT	CATTERMOLE	SCOTS DG
CAPT	COCHLAN	SCOTS DG
CAPT	CONNOR	SCOTS DG
CAPT	COSBY	1 IRISH GUARDS
CAPT	DAVIES	SCOTS DG
CAPT	DE SILVA	SCOTS DG
CAPT	DEVITT	1 IRISH GUARDS
CAPT	DOBESON	SCOTS DG
CAPT	FARRELL	31 ARMD ENGR SQN
CAPT	FOULERTON	SCOTS DG
CAPT	GARRAWAY	1 IRISH GUARDS
CAPT	GEMMELL	SCOTS DG
CAPT	HANLON	SCOTS DG
CAPT	HAWKINS	31 ARMD ENGR SQN
CAPT	HAYWARD	SCOTS DG
CAPT	HUBBARD	3 RHA
CAPT	JAMESON	SCOTS DG
CAPT	KERRIGAN	SCOTS DG
CAPT	LE SEUER	SCOTS DG
CAPT	LEEK	SCOTS DG
CAPT	LUCAS	SCOTS DG
CAPT	MACDERMOT-ROE	SCOTS DG
CAPT	MACKIE	SCOTS DG
CAPT	MACMILLAN	SCOTS DG
CAPT	MAGAN	1 IRISH GUARDS
CAPT	MALEC	3 RHA
CAPT	MATHESON	SCOTS DG
CAPT	MCLEMAN	SCOTS DG
CAPT	MICHAEL	31 ARMD ENGR SQN
CAPT	MORRISON	3 RHA
CAPT	MOULTON	1 IRISH GUARDS
CAPT	ONGARO	SCOTS DG
CAPT	POPE	SCOTS DG
CAPT	RICHARDSON	3 RHA
CAPT	ROGERS	SCOTS DG
CAPT	STEVENSON	SCOTS DG
CAPT	TOWARD	SCOTS DG
CAPT	TRUEMAN	SCOTS DG
CAPT	WADDIE	3 RHA
CAPT	WALTERS	SCOTS DG
CAPT	WILLIAMS	31 ARMD ENGR SQN
CAPT	WILLIAMSON	SCOTS DG
CAPT	WRIGHT	SCOTS DG
LT	COUPER-MARSH	31 ARMD ENGR SQN
LT	CRAIG	SCOTS DG
LT	DURDIN-ROBERTS	1 IRISH GUARDS
LT	JACK	SCOTS DG
LT	O'BRIEN	SCOTS DG
LT	O'CONNELL	1 IRISH GUARDS
LT	PLIMMER	31 ARMD ENGR SQN
LT	STONE	SCOTS DG
2LT	ALBERT	SCOTS DG
2LT	CHRISTIE	SCOTS DG
2LT	FERRIER	1 IRISH GUARDS
2LT	HAWLEY	1 IRISH GUARDS
2LT	LUCAS	SCOTS DG
2LT	MARJORIBANKS	SCOTS DG
2LT	ORDE-POWLETT	1 IRISH GUARDS
2LT	PLUMMER	1 IRISH GUARDS
2LT	THEOBALD	2 CS REGT RLC
WO1	EWING	SCOTS DG
WO1	O'CONNOR	SCOTS DG
WO2	ANDERSON	SCOTS DG
WO2	BARRON	31 ARMD ENGR SQN
WO2	BROTHERTON	SCOTS DG
WO2	DAMANT	1 IRISH GUARDS
WO2	DAVIDSON	SCOTS DG
WO2	GERAGHTY	1 IRISH GUARDS
WO2	GRAY	SCOTS DG
WO2	GREENWOOD	SCOTS DG
WO2	HARLEY	SCOTS DG
WO2	HARRIS	SCOTS DG
WO2	HAYES	SCOTS DG
WO2	MACINTYRE	SCOTS DG
WO2	MCDOWELL	SCOTS DG
WO2	SAUNDERS	SCOTS DG
WO2	SAXON	1 IRISH GUARDS
WO2	SHARPLES	SCOTS DG
WO2	SPENCE	SCOTS DG
WO2	STEVELY	SCOTS DG
WO2	WEBSTER	31 ARMD ENGR SQN
WO2	WHARTON	SCOTS DG
SSGT	ANDREWS	31 ARMD ENGR SQN
SSGT	BARCLAY	SCOTS DG
SSGT	BELL	SCOTS DG
SSGT	CROOT	SCOTS DG
SSGT	CROWHURST	31 ARMD ENGR SQN
SSGT	CURRIE	SCOTS DG
SSGT	DAVIES	3 RHA
SSGT	DELANEY	31 ARMD ENGR SQN
SSGT	EDWARDS	SCOTS DG
SSGT	GARDINER	SCOTS DG
SSGT	HANSON	SCOTS DG
SSGT	HENDERSON	SCOTS DG
SSGT	HINSON	SCOTS DG
SSGT	JOHNSTONE	SCOTS DG
SSGT	LEMMON	SCOTS DG
SSGT	LILLIE	SCOTS DG
SSGT	LITTLE	SCOTS DG
SSGT	LOCHRIE	SCOTS DG
SSGT	MARSHALL	31 ARMD ENGR SQN
SSGT	MCBEATH	SCOTS DG
SSGT	MCKENZIE	SCOTS DG
SSGT	MCVEY	SCOTS DG
SSGT	RAYNER	1 IRISH GUARDS
SSGT	REED	SCOTS DG
SSGT	RICHARDS	SCOTS DG
SSGT	RISEBOROUGH	31 ARMD ENGR SQN
SSGT	ROSS	SCOTS DG
SSGT	SHUGAR	31 ARMD ENGR SQN
SSGT	SIMPSON	SCOTS DG
SSGT	WALLACE	SCOTS DG
SSGT	WINDOW	SCOTS DG
CSGT	AIKEN	1 IRISH GUARDS
CSGT	CHARLES	1 IRISH GUARDS
CSGT	CRAWLEY	1 IRISH GUARDS
CSGT	EDWARDS	1 IRISH GUARDS
CSGT	FAGIN	1 IRISH GUARDS
CSGT	HARRIS	1 IRISH GUARDS
CSGT	HOWELL	1 IRISH GUARDS
CSGT	JOHNSON	1 IRISH GUARDS
CSGT	LALLY	1 IRISH GUARDS
CSGT	WATKINS	1 IRISH GUARDS
SGT	AVERY	3 RHA
SGT	BAIRD	SCOTS DG
SGT	BEVERIDGE	SCOTS DG
SGT	BEVERIDGE	SCOTS DG
SGT	BLAIR	SCOTS DG
SGT	BLAKE	SCOTS DG
SGT	BOYD	SCOTS DG
SGT	BRETTLE	1 IRISH GUARDS
SGT	BURDETT	SCOTS DG
SGT	CAMPBELL	1 IRISH GUARDS
SGT	CARTER	SCOTS DG
SGT	CLAYTON	SCOTS DG
SGT	CLEMMOW	SCOTS DG
SGT	COX	SCOTS DG
SGT	CRAWFORD	3 RHA
SGT	DALBY	SCOTS DG
SGT	DALE	1 IRISH GUARDS
SGT	DOBSON	31 ARMD ENGR SQN
SGT	DUDMAN	SCOTS DG
SGT	ENGLAND	SCOTS DG
SGT	ENGLAND	SCOTS DG
SGT	FERGUSON	SCOTS DG
SGT	FISHER	SCOTS DG
SGT	GAUGHAN	31 ARMD ENGR SQN
SGT	GIBBS	SCOTS DG
SGT	GRAY	SCOTS DG
SGT	HAINEY	SCOTS DG
SGT	HILTON	3 RHA
SGT	HUGILL	SCOTS DG
SGT	KAYE	SCOTS DG
SGT	LAMB	SCOTS DG
SGT	LATHAN	SCOTS DG
SGT	LEE	SCOTS DG
SGT	LITTLE	31 ARMD ENGR SQN
SGT	LOCKWOOD	SCOTS DG
SGT	LONG	SCOTS DG
SGT	MACDONALD	SCOTS DG
SGT	MACDONALD	SCOTS DG
SGT	MACK	SCOTS DG
SGT	MCCARTNEY	SCOTS DG
SGT	MCCLEERY	1 IRISH GUARDS
SGT	MCKELVIE	SCOTS DG
SGT	MCLAUGHLIN	SCOTS DG
SGT	MCQUISTON	2 CS REGT RLC
SGT	MONTGOMERY	SCOTS DG
SGT	NYE	31 ARMD ENGR SQN
SGT	O'CONNOR	SCOTS DG
SGT	PEARCE	SCOTS DG
SGT	PERRY	1 IRISH GUARDS
SGT	PICKFORD	1 IRISH GUARDS
SGT	POTTER	SCOTS DG
SGT	POTTER	SCOTS DG
SGT	RIELEY	SCOTS DG
SGT	ROBINS	SCOTS DG
SGT	RUSHTON	31 ARMD ENGR SQN
SGT	SHEPHARD	1 IRISH GUARDS
SGT	SMITH	SCOTS DG
SGT	SPEED	SCOTS DG
SGT	SPIBY	31 ARMD ENGR SQN
SGT	TAYLOR	SCOTS DG

Rank	Name	Unit	Rank	Name	Unit
SGT	TAYLOR	1 IRISH GUARDS	CPL	JOHNSTON	SCOTS DG
SGT	THOMAS	SCOTS DG	CPL	KENNAN	SCOTS DG
SGT	THOMPSON	1 IRISH GUARDS	CPL	LAVALLIN	SCOTS DG
SGT	THOMPSON	31 ARMD ENGR SQN	CPL	LEES	SCOTS DG
SGT	TODD	1 IRISH GUARDS	CPL	LENNOX	SCOTS DG
SGT	WALDEN	3 RHA	CPL	LOCKHART	SCOTS DG
SGT	WALKER	31 ARMD ENGR SQN	CPL	MACLEAN	SCOTS DG
SGT	WARING	1 IRISH GUARDS	CPL	MALCOLM	SCOTS DG
SGT	WATLING	1 IRISH GUARDS	CPL	MANSON	SCOTS DG
SGT	WATSON	SCOTS DG	CPL	MARNELL	SCOTS DG
SGT	WELSH	SCOTS DG	CPL	MASON	SCOTS DG
SGT	WHITESIDE	1 IRISH GUARDS	CPL	MATHEWS	SCOTS DG
SGT	WILSON	1 IRISH GUARDS	CPL	MCALISTER	SCOTS DG
SGT	WINTERS	SCOTS DG	CPL	MCCORMICK	SCOTS DG
SGT	WOOLEY	1 IRISH GUARDS	CPL	MCGEE	SCOTS DG
LSGT	AHERNE	1 IRISH GUARDS	CPL	MILLER	SCOTS DG
LSGT	BARKLE	1 IRISH GUARDS	CPL	MORRIS	SCOTS DG
LSGT	BEECH	1 IRISH GUARDS	CPL	NASH	SCOTS DG
LSGT	BRIGGS	1 IRISH GUARDS	CPL	NEWMAN	SCOTS DG
LSGT	BROOKS	1 IRISH GUARDS	CPL	O'DOWD	SCOTS DG
LSGT	BROWN	1 IRISH GUARDS	CPL	ORZEL	SCOTS DG
LSGT	BURNETT	1 IRISH GUARDS	CPL	PARKER	SCOTS DG
LSGT	BUTTERWORTH	1 IRISH GUARDS	CPL	PATERSON	SCOTS DG
LSGT	CHANEY	1 IRISH GUARDS	CPL	PATTERSON	SCOTS DG
LSGT	CHILTON	1 IRISH GUARDS	CPL	PATTINSON	SCOTS DG
LSGT	CLIFFORD	1 IRISH GUARDS	CPL	PELL	SCOTS DG
LSGT	CURRY	1 IRISH GUARDS	CPL	PERRY	SCOTS DG
LSGT	DEVINE	1 IRISH GUARDS	CPL	PRATT	SCOTS DG
LSGT	FARRELLY	1 IRISH GUARDS	CPL	RAMSAY	SCOTS DG
LSGT	FERGUSON	1 IRISH GUARDS	CPL	REID	SCOTS DG
LSGT	FLETCHER	1 IRISH GUARDS	CPL	RICHARDS	SCOTS DG
LSGT	GILES	1 IRISH GUARDS	CPL	RIGBY	SCOTS DG
LSGT	GRAY	1 IRISH GUARDS	CPL	ROBERTSON	SCOTS DG
LSGT	HANGER	1 IRISH GUARDS	CPL	ROSS	SCOTS DG
LSGT	HOBBS	1 IRISH GUARDS	CPL	ROSS	SCOTS DG
LSGT	HOCKING	1 IRISH GUARDS	CPL	ROSS	SCOTS DG
LSGT	HOGAN	1 IRISH GUARDS	CPL	SEXTON	SCOTS DG
LSGT	HOLLAND	1 IRISH GUARDS	CPL	SHAW	SCOTS DG
LSGT	HOOD	1 IRISH GUARDS	CPL	SHINKIN	SCOTS DG
LSGT	IRWIN	1 IRISH GUARDS	CPL	SILVESTER	SCOTS DG
LSGT	JACKSON	1 IRISH GUARDS	CPL	SIMONS	SCOTS DG
LSGT	JOHNSTON	1 IRISH GUARDS	CPL	SINCLAIR	SCOTS DG
LSGT	MCCONNELL	1 IRISH GUARDS	CPL	SKILLING	SCOTS DG
LSGT	MCGILLCUDDY	1 IRISH GUARDS	CPL	SMITH	SCOTS DG
LSGT	MCKERNAN	1 IRISH GUARDS	CPL	SMITH	SCOTS DG
LSGT	MOONEY	1 IRISH GUARDS	CPL	STEVENS	SCOTS DG
LSGT	OATLEY	1 IRISH GUARDS	CPL	SUTHERLAND	SCOTS DG
LSGT	O'CONNOR	1 IRISH GUARDS	CPL	TANNER	SCOTS DG
LSGT	PATTERSON	1 IRISH GUARDS	CPL	TAYLOR	SCOTS DG
LSGT	PURTELL	1 IRISH GUARDS	CPL	THOMAS	SCOTS DG
LSGT	ROSSITER	1 IRISH GUARDS	CPL	THOMSON	SCOTS DG
LSGT	RYAN	1 IRISH GUARDS	CPL	THORNTON	SCOTS DG
LSGT	SPENCER	1 IRISH GUARDS	CPL	THURSTON	SCOTS DG
LSGT	STEVENSON	1 IRISH GUARDS	CPL	TREADGOLD	SCOTS DG
LSGT	STEVENSON	1 IRISH GUARDS	CPL	VEITCH	SCOTS DG
LSGT	WADDELL	1 IRISH GUARDS	CPL	WALES	SCOTS DG
LSGT	WHITBY	1 IRISH GUARDS	CPL	WALLACE	SCOTS DG
LSGT	WRIGHT	1 IRISH GUARDS	CPL	WARD	SCOTS DG
CPL	ALLAN	SCOTS DG	CPL	WATERHOUSE	SCOTS DG
CPL	ASHER	SCOTS DG	CPL	WILSON	SCOTS DG
CPL	BALFOUR	SCOTS DG	LCPL	ADAMS	SCOTS DG
CPL	BEGGS	SCOTS DG	LCPL	ADEY	31 ARMD ENGR SQN
CPL	BEVAN	SCOTS DG	LCPL	AMES	1 IRISH GUARDS
CPL	BEVERIDGE	SCOTS DG	LCPL	ANDERSON	SCOTS DG
CPL	BEVERIDGE	SCOTS DG	LCPL	ANSELL	2 CS REGT RLC
CPL	BISHOP	31 ARMD ENGR SQN	LCPL	BARCLAY	SCOTS DG
CPL	BOWDEN	SCOTS DG	LCPL	BENZIE	31 ARMD ENGR SQN
CPL	BRAIN	SCOTS DG	LCPL	BEVERIDGE	SCOTS DG
CPL	BROWN	SCOTS DG	LCPL	BIRCH	31 ARMD ENGR SQN
CPL	BROWN	SCOTS DG	LCPL	BOYESON	SCOTS DG
CPL	CAMPBELL	SCOTS DG	LCPL	BRADFORD	1 IRISH GUARDS
CPL	CHARTERS	SCOTS DG	LCPL	BRANNIGAN	SCOTS DG
CPL	CHATFIELD	31 ARMD ENGR SQN	LCPL	BRENNAN	SCOTS DG
CPL	CHEETHAM	31 ARMD ENGR SQN	LCPL	BROWN	SCOTS DG
CPL	CHILTON	31 ARMD ENGR SQN	LCPL	BROWN	SCOTS DG
CPL	COOPER	SCOTS DG	LCPL	BRUCE	SCOTS DG
CPL	COULTER	SCOTS DG	LCPL	BRYAN	SCOTS DG
CPL	COWLE	2 RTR	LCPL	BURFORD	1 IRISH GUARDS
CPL	CRAMB	SCOTS DG	LCPL	BURGAN	1 IRISH GUARDS
CPL	CROCKETT	SCOTS DG	LCPL	BURROWS	SCOTS DG
CPL	DALE	SCOTS DG	LCPL	BURTON	1 IRISH GUARDS
CPL	DENNIS	SCOTS DG	LCPL	BURTON	1 IRISH GUARDS
CPL	DOUGAL	SCOTS DG	LCPL	BYRNE	1 IRISH GUARDS
CPL	DREVER	SCOTS DG	LCPL	CAMPBELL	1 IRISH GUARDS
CPL	DUDMAN	SCOTS DG	LCPL	CAMPBELL	SCOTS DG
CPL	EDWARDS	SCOTS DG	LCPL	CAREY	SCOTS DG
CPL	FINNIE	SCOTS DG	LCPL	CARPENTER	1 IRISH GUARDS
CPL	FORRESTER	SCOTS DG	LCPL	CASEY	1 IRISH GUARDS
CPL	GALLETLY	SCOTS DG	LCPL	CHALK	SCOTS DG
CPL	GARDINER	SCOTS DG	LCPL	CHANDLER	31 ARMD ENGR SQN
CPL	GARDINER	SCOTS DG	LCPL	CHART	SCOTS DG
CPL	GARRETT	SCOTS DG	LCPL	COPLEY	1 IRISH GUARDS
CPL	GIBBS	SCOTS DG	LCPL	COWAN	SCOTS DG
CPL	GILCHRIST	SCOTS DG	LCPL	COWIE	SCOTS DG
CPL	GOWANS	SCOTS DG	LCPL	CRESSEY	31 ARMD ENGR SQN
CPL	GOWLAND	SCOTS DG	LCPL	CRYSTAL	31 ARMD ENGR SQN
CPL	HAMILTON	SCOTS DG	LCPL	CUMMINGS	SCOTS DG
CPL	HENDRY	SCOTS DG	LCPL	DANIELS	SCOTS DG
CPL	HUGHESTON-ROB	SCOTS DG	LCPL	DARKE	SCOTS DG
CPL	INGHAM	SCOTS DG	LCPL	DAVIES	31 ARMD ENGR SQN
CPL	IRWIN	SCOTS DG	LCPL	DOCKREE	SCOTS DG
CPL	JAYS	SCOTS DG	LCPL	DODDS	SCOTS DG
			LCPL	DODDS	1 IRISH GUARDS

Rank	Name	Unit		Rank	Name	Unit
LCPL	DOWLING	1 IRISH GUARDS		LCPL	PERCY	SCOTS DG
LCPL	DRAPER	1 IRISH GUARDS		LCPL	PESCOD	SCOTS DG
LCPL	DRAPER	SCOTS DG		LCPL	PITTAM	1 IRISH GUARDS
LCPL	DRENNAN	1 IRISH GUARDS		LCPL	POWELL	1 IRISH GUARDS
LCPL	DUDLEY	SCOTS DG		LCPL	PRUETT	1 IRISH GUARDS
LCPL	DUFFY	SCOTS DG		LCPL	PURCELL	1 IRISH GUARDS
LCPL	DUFFY	1 IRISH GUARDS		LCPL	QUIN	SCOTS DG
LCPL	EDWARDS	1 IRISH GUARDS		LCPL	REID	SCOTS DG
LCPL	FAYE	1 IRISH GUARDS		LCPL	RENNIE	SCOTS DG
LCPL	FEATHERSTONE	SCOTS DG		LCPL	REYNOLDS	SCOTS DG
LCPL	FIELD	31 ARMD ENGR SQN		LCPL	REYNOLDS	SCOTS DG
LCPL	FLETCHER	SCOTS DG		LCPL	RICHARDS	31 ARMD ENGR SQN
LCPL	FORREST	31 ARMD ENGR SQN		LCPL	ROBERTSON	SCOTS DG
LCPL	FOX	31 ARMD ENGR SQN		LCPL	ROBINSON	1 IRISH GUARDS
LCPL	FRASER	SCOTS DG		LCPL	ROBINSON	31 ARMD ENGR SQN
LCPL	FRAZER	SCOTS DG		LCPL	ROBINSON	SCOTS DG
LCPL	GALLAGHER	SCOTS DG		LCPL	ROONEY	1 IRISH GUARDS
LCPL	GARRARD	31 ARMD ENGR SQN		LCPL	RUDDICK	1 IRISH GUARDS
LCPL	GIBSON	1 IRISH GUARDS		LCPL	SAGNIA	SCOTS DG
LCPL	GORE	SCOTS DG		LCPL	SCARFF	1 IRISH GUARDS
LCPL	GRIMES	31 ARMD ENGR SQN		LCPL	SCOULAR	SCOTS DG
LCPL	HAMILTON	1 IRISH GUARDS		LCPL	SHARPLES	1 IRISH GUARDS
LCPL	HAMILTON	SCOTS DG		LCPL	SHEEHAN	1 IRISH GUARDS
LCPL	HANNAH	1 IRISH GUARDS		LCPL	SMITH	SCOTS DG
LCPL	HARRIS	31 ARMD ENGR SQN		LCPL	SMITH	SCOTS DG
LCPL	HARRISON	SCOTS DG		LCPL	SNOXELL	SCOTS DG
LCPL	HARRY	1 IRISH GUARDS		LCPL	STARR	SCOTS DG
LCPL	HEMMINGS	1 IRISH GUARDS		LCPL	STEVENSON	SCOTS DG
LCPL	HENDEY	31 ARMD ENGR SQN		LCPL	STEVENSON	SCOTS DG
LCPL	HILL	31 ARMD ENGR SQN		LCPL	STIRLAND	31 ARMD ENGR SQN
LCPL	HINTON	SCOTS DG		LCPL	STORRIER	SCOTS DG
LCPL	HOLLENDER	1 IRISH GUARDS		LCPL	STRICKLAND	1 IRISH GUARDS
LCPL	HOLLIER	31 ARMD ENGR SQN		LCPL	TAYLOR	1 IRISH GUARDS
LCPL	HOOPER	SCOTS DG		LCPL	THOMASSON	31 ARMD ENGR SQN
LCPL	HORN	SCOTS DG		LCPL	THOMPSON	SCOTS DG
LCPL	HUGHES	SCOTS DG		LCPL	THORNTON	1 IRISH GUARDS
LCPL	HULL	1 IRISH GUARDS		LCPL	TOOMEY	SCOTS DG
LCPL	HUNTER	SCOTS DG		LCPL	TOPHAM	31 ARMD ENGR SQN
LCPL	JACKS	31 ARMD ENGR SQN		LCPL	TREADAWAY	31 ARMD ENGR SQN
LCPL	JACKSON	SCOTS DG		LCPL	UTTLEY	SCOTS DG
LCPL	JACKSON	1 IRISH GUARDS		LCPL	VANIQI	SCOTS DG
LCPL	JARDINE	1 IRISH GUARDS		LCPL	WAINWRIGHT	SCOTS DG
LCPL	JERVIS	1 IRISH GUARDS		LCPL	WALLACE	SCOTS DG
LCPL	JONES	31 ARMD ENGR SQN		LCPL	WEST	SCOTS DG
LCPL	JONES	SCOTS DG		LCPL	WHEATLEY	SCOTS DG
LCPL	KANE	SCOTS DG		LCPL	WHEELER	1 IRISH GUARDS
LCPL	KELLY	SCOTS DG		LCPL	WHELAN	SCOTS DG
LCPL	KHOO	SCOTS DG		LCPL	WHITE	1 IRISH GUARDS
LCPL	KINCH	31 ARMD ENGR SQN		LCPL	WHITE	1 IRISH GUARDS
LCPL	KING	SCOTS DG		LCPL	WILLIAMS	31 ARMD ENGR SQN
LCPL	KNIGHT	SCOTS DG		LCPL	WILLIAMS	1 IRISH GUARDS
LCPL	LAWSON	SCOTS DG		LCPL	WILLIAMS	1 IRISH GUARDS
LCPL	LENNOX	SCOTS DG		LCPL	WILLIAMS	1 IRISH GUARDS
LCPL	LESSELS	SCOTS DG		LCPL	WRIGHT	31 ARMD ENGR SQN
LCPL	LIVINGSTONE	SCOTS DG		LCPL	YORKE	SCOTS DG
LCPL	LLOYD	31 ARMD ENGR SQN		TPR	ABBOTT	SCOTS DG
LCPL	LOE	1 IRISH GUARDS		TPR	AH SING	SCOTS DG
LCPL	LOGUE	1 IRISH GUARDS		TPR	ALEXANDER	SCOTS DG
LCPL	LONGHURST	1 IRISH GUARDS		TPR	ARMSTRONG	SCOTS DG
LCPL	MACDONALD	SCOTS DG		TPR	BARTON	SCOTS DG
LCPL	MACFARLANE	SCOTS DG		TPR	BATIULUNA	SCOTS DG
LCPL	MACKENZIE	SCOTS DG		TPR	BESTWICK	SCOTS DG
LCPL	MACLEOD	SCOTS DG		TPR	BISHOP	SCOTS DG
LCPL	MACLEOD	1 IRISH GUARDS		TPR	BLACK	SCOTS DG
LCPL	MACRAE	SCOTS DG		TPR	BOATH	SCOTS DG
LCPL	MAIN	SCOTS DG		TPR	BOKAS	SCOTS DG
LCPL	MAJOR	1 IRISH GUARDS		TPR	BOYLE	SCOTS DG
LCPL	MALONE	1 IRISH GUARDS		TPR	BROWN	SCOTS DG
LCPL	MARTIN	SCOTS DG		TPR	BROWN	SCOTS DG
LCPL	MARTIN	1 IRISH GUARDS		TPR	BUDGEN	SCOTS DG
LCPL	MASON	SCOTS DG		TPR	BYRNE	SCOTS DG
LCPL	MAULE	SCOTS DG		TPR	CAMBRIDGE	SCOTS DG
LCPL	MCALEESE	SCOTS DG		TPR	CAMERON	SCOTS DG
LCPL	MCCALLUM	1 IRISH GUARDS		TPR	CASSIDY	SCOTS DG
LCPL	MCCHEYNE	SCOTS DG		TPR	CHANDLER	SCOTS DG
LCPL	MCCLEAN	SCOTS DG		TPR	CLEMENTS	SCOTS DG
LCPL	MCCLUSKEY	SCOTS DG		TPR	COLLIE	SCOTS DG
LCPL	MCCONNACHIE	SCOTS DG		TPR	CULLEN	SCOTS DG
LCPL	MCCREEDY	1 IRISH GUARDS		TPR	CULLEN	SCOTS DG
LCPL	MCCURDY	1 IRISH GUARDS		TPR	CUNNINGHAM	SCOTS DG
LCPL	MCCUSKER	SCOTS DG		TPR	DARLING	SCOTS DG
LCPL	MCDOUGALL	1 IRISH GUARDS		TPR	DAVIES	SCOTS DG
LCPL	MCMAHON	1 IRISH GUARDS		TPR	DE KLERK	SCOTS DG
LCPL	MCMENEMY	SCOTS DG		TPR	DEGEI	SCOTS DG
LCPL	MCPHEE	SCOTS DG		TPR	DOCHERTY	SCOTS DG
LCPL	MEAD	31 ARMD ENGR SQN		TPR	DOCHERTY	SCOTS DG
LCPL	MEIEHOFER	SCOTS DG		TPR	DODDS	SCOTS DG
LCPL	MILNER	SCOTS DG		TPR	DONNELLY	SCOTS DG
LCPL	MONTIETH	SCOTS DG		TPR	EMMERSON	SCOTS DG
LCPL	MORALEE	1 IRISH GUARDS		TPR	ENGLISH	SCOTS DG
LCPL	MORRIS	31 ARMD ENGR SQN		TPR	EVANS	SCOTS DG
LCPL	MORRISON	1 IRISH GUARDS		TPR	EVANSON	SCOTS DG
LCPL	MURPHY	1 IRISH GUARDS		TPR	FAIRBAIRN	SCOTS DG
LCPL	MUSSON	SCOTS DG		TPR	FERGUSON	SCOTS DG
LCPL	NEWTON	SCOTS DG		TPR	FERGUSON	SCOTS DG
LCPL	O'NEILL	1 IRISH GUARDS		TPR	FISHER	SCOTS DG
LCPL	O'NEILL	1 IRISH GUARDS		TPR	FITZGERALD	SCOTS DG
LCPL	O'SULLIVAN	1 IRISH GUARDS		TPR	FITZPATRICK	SCOTS DG
LCPL	O'SULLIVAN	1 IRISH GUARDS		TPR	FLEMING	SCOTS DG
LCPL	O'TOOLE	1 IRISH GUARDS		TPR	FORSYTH	SCOTS DG
LCPL	PAMMANT	1 IRISH GUARDS		TPR	FRASER	SCOTS DG
LCPL	PARKINSON	31 ARMD ENGR SQN		TPR	GILLON	SCOTS DG
LCPL	PARKINSON	1 IRISH GUARDS		TPR	GRANT	SCOTS DG

157

TPR	GREEN	SCOTS DG		TPR	TOUGHILL	SCOTS DG
TPR	GRIFFITHS	SCOTS DG		TPR	TUITUBOU	SCOTS DG
TPR	HACKING	SCOTS DG		TPR	URQUART	SCOTS DG
TPR	HALCROW	SCOTS DG		TPR	VULA	SCOTS DG
TPR	HARVEY	SCOTS DG		TPR	WALLACE	SCOTS DG
TPR	HAW	SCOTS DG		TPR	WHYTE	SCOTS DG
TPR	HEGARTY	SCOTS DG		TPR	WILLIAMSON	SCOTS DG
TPR	HERKES	SCOTS DG		TPR	WILLIAMSON	SCOTS DG
TPR	HOGG	SCOTS DG		TPR	WOODCOCK	SCOTS DG
TPR	HOPE	SCOTS DG		TPR	YATES	SCOTS DG
TPR	HUNTER	SCOTS DG		TPR	YOUNG	SCOTS DG
TPR	IMRIE	SCOTS DG		TPR	YOUNG	SCOTS DG
TPR	JACK	SCOTS DG		TPR	YOUNGMAN	SCOTS DG
TPR	JACKSON	SCOTS DG		TPR	YOUNGMAN	SCOTS DG
TPR	JENKINS	SCOTS DG		BDR	ALDRIDGE	3 RHA
TPR	JOHNSTONE	SCOTS DG		BDR	CLARKE	3 RHA
TPR	KEITH	SCOTS DG		BDR	DUNN	3 RHA
TPR	KELLY	SCOTS DG		BDR	FORSYTH	3 RHA
TPR	KELLY	SCOTS DG		BDR	HUNT	3 RHA
TPR	KETEDROMO	SCOTS DG		BDR	KINGHORN	3 RHA
TPR	LECKIE	SCOTS DG		BDR	TORRANCE	3 RHA
TPR	LEYDEN	SCOTS DG		LBDR	CLARK	3 RHA
TPR	LLOYD	SCOTS DG		LBDR	COTTERALL	3 RHA
TPR	LOAGE	SCOTS DG		LBDR	JEFFRIES	3 RHA
TPR	LOFTUS	SCOTS DG		LBDR	JONES	3 RHA
TPR	LOMALAGI	SCOTS DG		LBDR	JONES	3 RHA
TPR	LOVELL	SCOTS DG		LBDR	WAREING	3 RHA
TPR	LYNN	SCOTS DG		GNR	HILTON	3 RHA
TPR	MACAWAI	SCOTS DG		GNR	HOLT	3 RHA
TPR	MACDONALD	SCOTS DG		SPR	ADAMS	31 ARMD ENGR SQN
TPR	MACMASTER	SCOTS DG		SPR	BARKER	31 ARMD ENGR SQN
TPR	MACRAE	SCOTS DG		SPR	BARNES	31 ARMD ENGR SQN
TPR	MAHER	SCOTS DG		SPR	BLACKIE	31 ARMD ENGR SQN
TPR	MANCHESTER	SCOTS DG		SPR	BOOTH	31 ARMD ENGR SQN
TPR	MANNERS	SCOTS DG		SPR	BULLARD	31 ARMD ENGR SQN
TPR	MATAGASAU	SCOTS DG		SPR	BUSSEY	31 ARMD ENGR SQN
TPR	MATE	SCOTS DG		SPR	CAMPBELL	31 ARMD ENGR SQN
TPR	MATHESON	SCOTS DG		SPR	CARTER	31 ARMD ENGR SQN
TPR	MATTHIES	SCOTS DG		SPR	CRAIG	31 ARMD ENGR SQN
TPR	MCBETH	SCOTS DG		SPR	CUBBAGE	31 ARMD ENGR SQN
TPR	MCBRIDE	SCOTS DG		SPR	CULLNEAN	31 ARMD ENGR SQN
TPR	MCCAFFERTY	SCOTS DG		SPR	DIXON	31 ARMD ENGR SQN
TPR	MCCALL	SCOTS DG		SPR	DOGGETT	31 ARMD ENGR SQN
TPR	MCCALL	SCOTS DG		SPR	DOSUNMU	31 ARMD ENGR SQN
TPR	MCCALL	SCOTS DG		SPR	DOUGLAS	31 ARMD ENGR SQN
TPR	MCCANN	SCOTS DG		SPR	DOWNWARD	31 ARMD ENGR SQN
TPR	MCINALLY	SCOTS DG		SPR	EMERTON	31 ARMD ENGR SQN
TPR	MCINTYRE	SCOTS DG		SPR	EVANS	31 ARMD ENGR SQN
TPR	MCKICHAN	SCOTS DG		SPR	GROTTICK	31 ARMD ENGR SQN
TPR	MCLARDIE	SCOTS DG		SPR	HARVEY	31 ARMD ENGR SQN
TPR	MCLAUCHLAN	SCOTS DG		SPR	HUGHES	31 ARMD ENGR SQN
TPR	MCLEOD	SCOTS DG		SPR	IRELAND	31 ARMD ENGR SQN
TPR	MCMINN	SCOTS DG		SPR	JOBLING	31 ARMD ENGR SQN
TPR	MCRITCHIE	SCOTS DG		SPR	KELLARY	31 ARMD ENGR SQN
TPR	MCSEVENLEY	SCOTS DG		SPR	KELLETT	31 ARMD ENGR SQN
TPR	MILLAR	SCOTS DG		SPR	LAWRENCE	31 ARMD ENGR SQN
TPR	MILLER	SCOTS DG		SPR	MCCAIRN	31 ARMD ENGR SQN
TPR	MINNOCK	SCOTS DG		SPR	MCCANN	31 ARMD ENGR SQN
TPR	MITCHELL	SCOTS DG		SPR	MCLACHLAN	31 ARMD ENGR SQN
TPR	MONAGHAN	SCOTS DG		SPR	MCLAUGHLIN	31 ARMD ENGR SQN
TPR	MORGAN	SCOTS DG		SPR	MOONEY	31 ARMD ENGR SQN
TPR	MORGAN-WILLIAMS	SCOTS DG		SPR	MORLEY	31 ARMD ENGR SQN
TPR	MORRISON	SCOTS DG		SPR	PARTRIDGE	31 ARMD ENGR SQN
TPR	MULLEN	SCOTS DG		SPR	PHILPS	31 ARMD ENGR SQN
TPR	MUNRO	SCOTS DG		SPR	PLEDGER	31 ARMD ENGR SQN
TPR	NAILATICA	SCOTS DG		SPR	SELMAN	1 IRISH GUARDS
TPR	NEAT	SCOTS DG		SPR	SEYMOUR	31 ARMD ENGR SQN
TPR	NORTON	SCOTS DG		SPR	SLOAN	31 ARMD ENGR SQN
TPR	O'DONNELL	SCOTS DG		SPR	STEVENS	31 ARMD ENGR SQN
TPR	PAGE	SCOTS DG		SPR	TAIT	31 ARMD ENGR SQN
TPR	PARKER	SCOTS DG		SPR	TRIGGS	31 ARMD ENGR SQN
TPR	PARKINSON	SCOTS DG		SPR	TULLY	31 ARMD ENGR SQN
TPR	PETRIE	SCOTS DG		SPR	WALDRON	31 ARMD ENGR SQN
TPR	PINCOTT	SCOTS DG		SPR	WALLS	31 ARMD ENGR SQN
TPR	PRENTICE	SCOTS DG		SPR	WALTON	31 ARMD ENGR SQN
TPR	PROSSER	SCOTS DG		SPR	WATSON	31 ARMD ENGR SQN
TPR	QUINN	SCOTS DG		SPR	WHITE	31 ARMD ENGR SQN
TPR	RAE	SCOTS DG		SPR	WILLIAMS	31 ARMD ENGR SQN
TPR	RAVUNAMELO	SCOTS DG		SPR	WINFIELD	31 ARMD ENGR SQN
TPR	REID	SCOTS DG		LCPL	ASHFORD	1 IRISH GUARDS
TPR	REID	SCOTS DG		LCPL	BAILEY	SCOTS DG
TPR	REID	SCOTS DG		LCPL	BAXTER	1 IRISH GUARDS
TPR	REID	SCOTS DG		LCPL	BELL	31 ARMD ENGR SQN
TPR	RIDYARD	SCOTS DG		LCPL	BICKERTON	SCOTS DG
TPR	ROKOBUTABUTA	SCOTS DG		LCPL	BOYLE	SCOTS DG
TPR	RUSSELL	SCOTS DG		LCPL	BRACKENBURY	SCOTS DG
TPR	RUSSELL	SCOTS DG		LCPL	BROWN	SCOTS DG
TPR	SAULAILAI	SCOTS DG		LCPL	BURRELL	SCOTS DG
TPR	SCALLY	SCOTS DG		LCPL	BUSH	31 ARMD ENGR SQN
TPR	SCOTT	SCOTS DG		LCPL	CAVENEY	31 ARMD ENGR SQN
TPR	SCOTT	SCOTS DG		LCPL	COX	SCOTS DG
TPR	SEBOK	SCOTS DG		LCPL	CRICHTON	31 ARMD ENGR SQN
TPR	SENIOR	SCOTS DG		LCPL	CUPPLES	SCOTS DG
TPR	SLOWE	SCOTS DG		LCPL	DALE	SCOTS DG
TPR	SMITH	SCOTS DG		LCPL	DAVIES	SCOTS DG
TPR	SOUTH	SCOTS DG		LCPL	DAVIS	31 ARMD ENGR SQN
TPR	STEEL	SCOTS DG		LCPL	DOYLE	SCOTS DG
TPR	STEVENSON	SCOTS DG		LCPL	DURRANT	SCOTS DG
TPR	STEVENSON	SCOTS DG		LCPL	EVANS	1 IRISH GUARDS
TPR	STEWART	SCOTS DG		LCPL	FOYLE	1 IRISH GUARDS
TPR	STORR	SCOTS DG		LCPL	GIBSON	SCOTS DG
TPR	THORBURN	SCOTS DG		LCPL	HAYLETT	1 IRISH GUARDS
TPR	TODD	SCOTS DG		LCPL	HIGINBOTHAM	SCOTS DG

Rank	Name	Unit
LCPL	MEAD	SCOTS DG
LCPL	MEAGER	SCOTS DG
LCPL	MEFFEN	SCOTS DG
LCPL	NAMUDU	SCOTS DG
LCPL	O'NEILL	SCOTS DG
LCPL	PEARCE	SCOTS DG
LCPL	SHANNON	31 ARMD ENGR SQN
LCPL	SHARPLES	SCOTS DG
LCPL	SINGER	SCOTS DG
LCPL	SMITH	SCOTS DG
LCPL	SPENCE	SCOTS DG
LCPL	STRONG	1 IRISH GUARDS
LCPL	TAVAINAVESI	31 ARMD ENGR SQN
LCPL	VAMARASI	SCOTS DG
LCPL	WHOPPLES	SCOTS DG
DMR	EDGAR	1 IRISH GUARDS
DMR	HILL	1 IRISH GUARDS
DMR	JONES	1 IRISH GUARDS
PPR	DUDDY	1 IRISH GUARDS
CPL	ARCHIBALD	1 IRISH GUARDS
CPL	COLLINS	1 IRISH GUARDS
CPL	CONSTANTINE	31 ARMD ENGR SQN
CPL	COX	SCOTS DG
CPL	ELLIS	31 ARMD ENGR SQN
CPL	FISHER	1 IRISH GUARDS
CPL	GIBBON	31 ARMD ENGR SQN
CPL	GOTSELL	31 ARMD ENGR SQN
CPL	HEWARD	31 ARMD ENGR SQN
CPL	LEITHER	31 ARMD ENGR SQN
CPL	MARSH	31 ARMD ENGR SQN
CPL	MOGER	31 ARMD ENGR SQN
CPL	PARR	31 ARMD ENGR SQN
CPL	PAUL	31 ARMD ENGR SQN
CPL	REED	1 IRISH GUARDS
CPL	SKELLY	31 ARMD ENGR SQN
CPL	SPARKS	31 ARMD ENGR SQN
CPL	TINNION	31 ARMD ENGR SQN
CPL	VALLELY	31 ARMD ENGR SQN
CPL	WALSH	31 ARMD ENGR SQN
CPL	WOODLEY	31 ARMD ENGR SQN
PTE	CASSIDY	SCOTS DG
PTE	DURU	SCOTS DG
PTE	EDWARDS	2 CS REGT RLC
PTE	HALLSWORTH	SCOTS DG
PTE	HUMPHRIES	SCOTS DG
PTE	LATHAM	2 CS REGT RLC
PTE	MASON LAMB	SCOTS DG
PTE	MILCZAREK	1 IRISH GUARDS
PTE	RICHARDS	1 IRISH GUARDS
PTE	TURNER	1 IRISH GUARDS
PTE	TURNER	1 IRISH GUARDS
PTE	WITT	SCOTS DG
GDSM	ALLEN	1 IRISH GUARDS
GDSM	ARMSTRONG	1 IRISH GUARDS
GDSM	BALL	1 IRISH GUARDS
GDSM	BELL	1 IRISH GUARDS
GDSM	BIRNIE	1 IRISH GUARDS
GDSM	BLAKEWAY	1 IRISH GUARDS
GDSM	BLAKEWAY	1 IRISH GUARDS
GDSM	BOJANG	1 IRISH GUARDS
GDSM	BOURN	1 IRISH GUARDS
GDSM	BOYD	1 IRISH GUARDS
GDSM	BRANCHFLOWER	1 IRISH GUARDS
GDSM	BRANNIGAN	1 IRISH GUARDS
GDSM	BREEN	1 IRISH GUARDS
GDSM	BROWN	1 IRISH GUARDS
GDSM	BROWN	1 IRISH GUARDS
GDSM	BULL-EDWARDS	1 IRISH GUARDS
GDSM	BURROUGHS	1 IRISH GUARDS
GDSM	BYRNE	1 IRISH GUARDS
GDSM	BYRNE	1 IRISH GUARDS
GDSM	CAMPBELL	1 IRISH GUARDS
GDSM	CASH	1 IRISH GUARDS
GDSM	CASTLE	1 IRISH GUARDS
GDSM	CATTELL	1 IRISH GUARDS
GDSM	CAUGHERS	1 IRISH GUARDS
GDSM	CHARLTON	1 IRISH GUARDS
GDSM	COBURN	1 IRISH GUARDS
GDSM	COCHRANE	1 IRISH GUARDS
GDSM	CONNELLY	1 IRISH GUARDS
GDSM	COOK	1 IRISH GUARDS
GDSM	COOKE	1 IRISH GUARDS
GDSM	COOKE	1 IRISH GUARDS
GDSM	COTTIS	1 IRISH GUARDS
GDSM	CROSSLEY	1 IRISH GUARDS
GDSM	CULBERTSON	1 IRISH GUARDS
GDSM	CUNNINGHAM	1 IRISH GUARDS
GDSM	DAVIES	1 IRISH GUARDS
GDSM	DAY	1 IRISH GUARDS
GDSM	DEVLIN	1 IRISH GUARDS
GDSM	EAMES	1 IRISH GUARDS
GDSM	ENWRIGHT	1 IRISH GUARDS
GDSM	ESTIEN	1 IRISH GUARDS
GDSM	EVANS	1 IRISH GUARDS
GDSM	FLEMING	1 IRISH GUARDS
GDSM	GARDINER	1 IRISH GUARDS
GDSM	GOUCHER	1 IRISH GUARDS
GDSM	HALL	1 IRISH GUARDS
GDSM	HARRIS	1 IRISH GUARDS
GDSM	HARRIS	1 IRISH GUARDS
GDSM	HARRIS	1 IRISH GUARDS
GDSM	HARTLEY	1 IRISH GUARDS
GDSM	HEANEY	1 IRISH GUARDS
GDSM	HENRY	1 IRISH GUARDS
GDSM	HERRITY	1 IRISH GUARDS
GDSM	HESSION	1 IRISH GUARDS
GDSM	HOGG	1 IRISH GUARDS
GDSM	HOLGATE	1 IRISH GUARDS
GDSM	HUGHES	1 IRISH GUARDS
GDSM	HUNTER	1 IRISH GUARDS
GDSM	JENKINS	1 IRISH GUARDS
GDSM	JOHNSTON	1 IRISH GUARDS
GDSM	JONES	1 IRISH GUARDS
GDSM	KENDAL	1 IRISH GUARDS
GDSM	KERR	1 IRISH GUARDS
GDSM	KING	1 IRISH GUARDS
GDSM	KITTO	1 IRISH GUARDS
GDSM	KLIEVE	1 IRISH GUARDS
GDSM	LASISI	1 IRISH GUARDS
GDSM	LAVERTY	1 IRISH GUARDS
GDSM	LESUBULA	1 IRISH GUARDS
GDSM	LEVERTON	1 IRISH GUARDS
GDSM	LOGUE	1 IRISH GUARDS
GDSM	MACMILLAN	1 IRISH GUARDS
GDSM	MAGILL	1 IRISH GUARDS
GDSM	MALONEY	1 IRISH GUARDS
GDSM	MARSH	1 IRISH GUARDS
GDSM	MARSHALL	1 IRISH GUARDS
GDSM	MARTINEZ	1 IRISH GUARDS
GDSM	MAWHINNEY	1 IRISH GUARDS
GDSM	MCCABE	1 IRISH GUARDS
GDSM	MCCLAY	1 IRISH GUARDS
GDSM	MCCLEARY	1 IRISH GUARDS
GDSM	MCDERMOTT-WIL	1 IRISH GUARDS
GDSM	MCDONOUGH	1 IRISH GUARDS
GDSM	MCGING	1 IRISH GUARDS
GDSM	MCKENZIE	1 IRISH GUARDS
GDSM	MCLAUGHLIN	1 IRISH GUARDS
GDSM	MCNEILL	1 IRISH GUARDS
GDSM	MCWILLIAMS	1 IRISH GUARDS
GDSM	MCWIRTER	1 IRISH GUARDS
GDSM	MEAD	1 IRISH GUARDS
GDSM	MEALIN	1 IRISH GUARDS
GDSM	MELIA	1 IRISH GUARDS
GDSM	MELLORS	1 IRISH GUARDS
GDSM	MORAN	1 IRISH GUARDS
GDSM	MUZVURU	1 IRISH GUARDS
GDSM	NAGERA	1 IRISH GUARDS
GDSM	NASH	1 IRISH GUARDS
GDSM	NAVUNI	1 IRISH GUARDS
GDSM	NEWMAN	1 IRISH GUARDS
GDSM	NIBLETT	1 IRISH GUARDS
GDSM	NICHOLSON	1 IRISH GUARDS
GDSM	O'CONNOR	1 IRISH GUARDS
GDSM	ODDY	1 IRISH GUARDS
GDSM	OLIVER	1 IRISH GUARDS
GDSM	PARFITT	1 IRISH GUARDS
GDSM	PERRY	1 IRISH GUARDS
GDSM	PHILLIPS	1 IRISH GUARDS
GDSM	PINTAR	1 IRISH GUARDS
GDSM	PROCTOR	1 IRISH GUARDS
GDSM	QUINN	1 IRISH GUARDS
GDSM	RICHARDS	1 IRISH GUARDS
GDSM	RICHARDSON	1 IRISH GUARDS
GDSM	RODGERS	1 IRISH GUARDS
GDSM	ROGERS	1 IRISH GUARDS
GDSM	RUSH	1 IRISH GUARDS
GDSM	SAINT	1 IRISH GUARDS
GDSM	SALTHOUSE	1 IRISH GUARDS
GDSM	SAMPAT	1 IRISH GUARDS
GDSM	SERSA	1 IRISH GUARDS
GDSM	SHAW	1 IRISH GUARDS
GDSM	SHEEHY	1 IRISH GUARDS
GDSM	SIMMS	1 IRISH GUARDS
GDSM	SLATER	1 IRISH GUARDS
GDSM	SMITH	1 IRISH GUARDS
GDSM	SMITHSON	1 IRISH GUARDS
GDSM	STEWART	1 IRISH GUARDS
GDSM	STORER	1 IRISH GUARDS
GDSM	STOTT	1 IRISH GUARDS
GDSM	STRANIX	1 IRISH GUARDS
GDSM	SUCKLING	1 IRISH GUARDS
GDSM	SUTTILL	1 IRISH GUARDS
GDSM	TAYLOR	1 IRISH GUARDS
GDSM	TESTER	1 IRISH GUARDS
GDSM	THORNTON	1 IRISH GUARDS
GDSM	TODD	1 IRISH GUARDS
GDSM	TOMLINSON	1 IRISH GUARDS
GDSM	TRAVIS	1 IRISH GUARDS
GDSM	TROWMANS	1 IRISH GUARDS
GDSM	WAITE	1 IRISH GUARDS
GDSM	WALKER	1 IRISH GUARDS
GDSM	WALKER	1 IRISH GUARDS
GDSM	WAQALEVU	1 IRISH GUARDS
GDSM	WARD	1 IRISH GUARDS
GDSM	WARD	1 IRISH GUARDS
GDSM	WHEELER	1 IRISH GUARDS
GDSM	WHITE	1 IRISH GUARDS
GDSM	WILKINS	1 IRISH GUARDS
GDSM	WILLIAMS	1 IRISH GUARDS
GDSM	WILSON	1 IRISH GUARDS
GDSM	WITHEY	1 IRISH GUARDS
GDSM	WOODS	1 IRISH GUARDS
GDSM	WUNDERLEY	1 IRISH GUARDS

MAJOR AIDAN STEPHEN was born in Edinburgh in 1970. He joined the Regiment in 1992, serving on operations in Bosnia, Northern Ireland, Kosovo and Iraq.

During the war, he held the appointment of Battlegroup Warfare Officer then Civilian Liaison Officer after the liberation of Basrah. He has recently taken up appointment as B Squadron Leader.

Although a keen artist, he had never been interested in photography but is now an enthusiastic amateur. He took a Fuji 602 Zoom Digital camera to Iraq and took photographs for the Battlegroup whenever he could. He is married to Amy and has a Springer Spaniel called Piper.

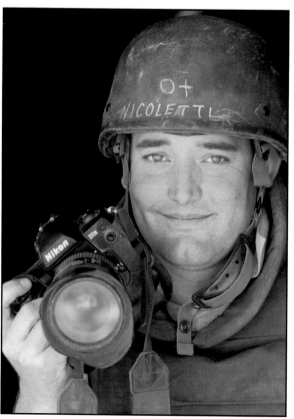

TONY NICOLETTI was born in Glasgow in 1976. He studied photography at college in Glasgow and became a professional photographer in 1994.

He has covered stories in all parts of the world – in Kosovo, Africa, Israel, Argentina and was sent to New York to cover the aftermath of September 11th.

He has worked for the Daily Record since 1997 and was sent to Iraq as an embedded journalist with The Royal Scots Dragoon Guards Battlegroup. His pictures were taken on two Nikon D1H digital cameras with various Nikkor lenses. Many of his images were sent back by satellite and used in papers all over the world. He is a day skipper and a keen fly fisherman.

THIRSTY WORK

Back cover: Dust settles on the Adjutant's glasses (see Page 71)

This book could not have been produced without the backing of our sponsors: